The Homen Chocolate Truttle Cookbook

Delicious and Easy Truffle Recipes

By
BookSumo Press
All rights reserved

Published by
http://www.booksumo.com

ENJOY THE RECIPES?

KEEP ON COOKING WITH 6 MORE FREE COOKBOOKS!

Click the link below and simply enter your email address to join the club and receive your 6 cookbooks.

http://booksumo.com/magnet

 https://www.instagram.com/booksumopress/

 https://www.facebook.com/booksumo/

LEGAL NOTES

All Rights Reserved. No Part Of This Book May Be Reproduced Or Transmitted In Any Form Or By Any Means. Photocopying, Posting Online, And / Or Digital Copying Is Strictly Prohibited Unless Written Permission Is Granted By The Book's Publishing Company. Limited Use Of The Book's Text Is Permitted For Use In Reviews Written For The Public.

Table of Contents

5......Truffles 101
6......Almond Wafer Truffles
7......Christmas Truffles
8......Cake Crumb Truffles
9......Coffee Chocolate Truffles
10......Cocoa Truffle Cookies
11......3-Ingredient Truffles
12......White Chocolate Truffles
13......Shredded Coconut Truffles
14......Orange Fruitcake Truffles
15......Peanut Butter Truffles
16......Cream Cheese Vanilla Truffles
17......Whipped Cream Cookie Truffle Pie
18......Expresso Truffles
19......Potluck Truffles
20......Mediterranean Almond Truffles
21......December's Peppermint Truffles
22......Simple Truffle Torte
23......Raisins, Cranberry, and Plum Truffles
24......I ♥ Truffles
25......Raspberry Truffle Fudge
26......Apricot Cinnamon Truffles
27......Southern Jam Truffles
28......Hazelnut Truffle Cupcakes
29......Carolina Sunflower Truffles
30......Pecan Truffles
31......Moe's Favorite Truffles
32......Almond Bark Truffles
33......Chive Truffles
34......Nutella Truffles
36......Venus Truffles
38......True Italian Truffles
40......Truffled Cheesecake
41......Gourmet Truffles
42......Glamorous ★Truffles★
43......Restaurant Style Truffles
44......French Truffles
45......Truffle Icing
46......Truffles Forever
47......Truffles Combo
48......Fathia's Truffles

Truffles 101

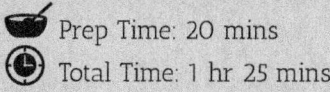

Prep Time: 20 mins
Total Time: 1 hr 25 mins

Servings per Recipe: 42
Calories   119 kcal
Fat   7.4 g
Carbohydrates   13g
Protein   1.7 g
Cholesterol   6 mg
Sodium   61 mg

Ingredients

1 (14 oz.) package chocolate sandwich cookies
1 (8 oz.) package cream cheese, cubed and softened
1 lb. semisweet chocolate, chopped
1 tbsp shortening

Directions

1. Line a baking sheet with a wax paper.
2. In a food processor, add the chocolate sandwich cookies and pulse till a fine crumb forms.
3. Reserve about 1/2 C. of the crumbs in a small bowl.
4. In the food processor, add the cream cheese with the remaining crumbs and pulse till well combined.
5. Make walnut-size balls from the mixture.
6. In a microwave-safe glass bowl, add the chocolate and shortening and melt in 30-second intervals, stirring after each melting, for about 1-3 minutes.
7. Coat the balls with the chocolate mixture evenly.
8. With 2 forks, lift the truffles out of the chocolate mixture, letting excess chocolate drip into the bowl.
9. Transfer the truffles onto the prepared baking sheet.
10. Immediately sprinkle the reserved cookie crumbs over the truffles.
11. Refrigerate to chill for about 1 hour.

ALMOND WAFER
Truffles

Prep Time: 15 mins
Total Time: 1 hr 50 mins

Servings per Recipe: 48
Calories   103 kcal
Fat   5.3 g
Carbohydrates   13g
Protein   1.4 g
Cholesterol   0 mg
Sodium   36 mg

Ingredients

- 1 1/4 C. almonds
- 2 1/2 C. crushed vanilla wafers
- 1/2 C. confectioners' sugar
- 2 tsp ground cinnamon
- 1 C. semi-sweet chocolate chips, melted
- 1/2 C. pumpkin puree (such as Libby's(R))
- 1/3 C. strong brewed coffee
- 1/2 C. semi-sweet chocolate chips, or as needed

Directions

1. Set your oven to 400 degrees F before doing anything else.
2. Spread the almonds onto a baking sheet and cook in the oven for about 5-10 minutes.
3. Remove from the oven and keep aside to cool completely.
4. In a food processor, add the almonds and pulse till a flour-like texture forms.
5. In a bowl, mix together the ground almonds, crushed vanilla wafers, confectioners' sugar and cinnamon.
6. Stir in 1 C. of the melted chocolate chips, pumpkin and coffee.
7. Make abut 1-inch balls from the mixture and place onto a baking sheet.
8. Refrigerate the truffles for about 1-2 hours.
9. In the top of a double boiler, melt 1/2 C. of the chocolate chips over simmering water, stirring occasionally. a
10. Dip truffles in melted chocolate and return to baking sheet to harden.

Christmas
Truffles

🥣 Prep Time: 25 mins
🕐 Total Time: 4 hr

Servings per Recipe: 16
Calories   125 kcal
Fat   9.1 g
Carbohydrates   10.3g
Protein   1.4 g
Cholesterol   11 mg
Sodium   13 mg

Ingredients

12 fresh lavender flower heads
1/3 C. heavy cream
6 oz. bittersweet chocolate, chopped
4 oz. semisweet chocolate, chopped
2 tbsp unsalted butter

Directions

1. In a small microwave safe glass bowl, place the cream and lavender heads and microwave on High for about 20-30 seconds.
2. Add the lavender and stir to combine, then keep aside for about 5 minutes to steep.
3. Return to the microwave, and cook for about 10-20 seconds.
4. Stir again, and keep aside for about 5 minutes to steep.
5. Repeat the heating-stirring-steeping process two more times until the cream is strongly flavored with lavender.
6. In a bowl, mix together both the chocolates.
7. Transfer half of the chocolate mixture in a microwave safe glass bowl and microwave on High for about 20-30 second increments until melted, stirring between each heating.
8. With a fine-mesh strainer, strain the cream into the melted chocolate and discard the flower heads and bits of lavender.
9. Refrigerator to chill for about 1 hour.
10. After chilling, place the remaining chocolate and butter into a microwave safe glass bowl and microwave on High for about 20-30 second increments until just melted, stirring between each heating.
11. Line a baking sheet with a waxed paper.
12. Make small equal sized balls with 1 tbsp of the lavender mixture and roll into the melted chocolate mixture evenly.
13. Arrange the balls onto the prepared baking sheet and refrigerator to chill for at least 2 hours.

CAKE
Crumb Truffles

🥣 Prep Time: 10 mins
🕐 Total Time: 1 hr 50 mins

Servings per Recipe: 24
Calories   98 kcal
Fat   6.2 g
Carbohydrates   9.6g
Protein   0.9 g
Cholesterol   8 mg
Sodium   9 mg

Ingredients

8 (1 oz.) squares bittersweet chocolate, chopped
1/4 C. cream
2 tbsp unsalted butter
1/2 C. chocolate cake crumbs
2 tsp apple juice, optional

1/2 C. chocolate sprinkles

Directions

1. Line a sheet pan with a parchment paper.
2. In a heatproof bowl, place the chopped chocolate.
3. In a pan, mix together the cream and butter on low heat and bring to a boil.
4. Place the hot cream mixture over the chocolate and stir till the chocolate is melted and smooth.
5. Stir in the cake crumbs and apple juice and keep aside till firm, but not hard.
6. With a heaping tsp of the chocolate mixture, make the balls and then coat with the chocolate sprinkles.
7. Place on the prepared sheet pan and refrigerate for about 30 minutes.
8. Serve in small paper cups.

Coffee Chocolate Truffles

Prep Time: 20 mins
Total Time: 2 hr 35 mins

Servings per Recipe: 66
Calories   75 kcal
Fat   5.3 g
Carbohydrates   8g
Protein   0.9 g
Cholesterol   4 mg
Sodium   11 mg

Ingredients

Truffle:
1 (24 oz.) bag semi-sweet chocolate chips
8 oz. cream cheese, softened
3 tbsp instant coffee granules
2 tsp water
Coating:
6 oz. semi-sweet chocolate chips

1 tbsp shortening

Directions

1. Line a baking sheet with a wax paper.
2. In a microwave safe bowl, melt 24 oz. chocolate chips in 30-second intervals, stirring after each melting for about 1-3 minutes.
3. Add the cream cheese, coffee granules and water into the melted chocolate and mix till smooth.
4. Refrigerate to chill the chocolate mixture for about 30 minutes.
5. Make about 1-inch balls from the chocolate mixture and place on the prepared baking sheet.
6. Refrigerate to chill for at least 1-2 hours.
7. In a microwave-safe glass bowl, melt 6 oz. chocolate chips and shortening in 30-second intervals, stirring after each melting, for about 1-3 minutes.
8. Coat the truffles in the melted chocolate mixture and arrange into the prepared baking sheet.
9. Keep aside for at least 30 minutes.

COCOA
Truffle Cookies

Prep Time: 15 mins
Total Time: 2 hr

Servings per Recipe: 36
Calories 112 kcal
Fat 6.8 g
Carbohydrates 13.9 g
Protein 1.6 g
Cholesterol 21 mg
Sodium 40 mg

Ingredients

4 (1 oz.) squares unsweetened chocolate, chopped
1 C. semisweet chocolate chips
6 tbsp butter
3 eggs
1 C. white sugar
1 1/2 tsp vanilla extract
1/2 C. all-purpose flour
2 tbsp unsweetened cocoa powder
1/4 tsp baking powder
1/4 tsp salt
1 C. semisweet chocolate chips

Directions

1. In a metal bowl, add the unsweetened chocolate, 1 C. of the chocolate chips and the butter over a pan of simmering water, stirring occasionally till smooth.
2. Remove from the heat and keep aside to cool.
3. In a large bowl, add the eggs and sugar and beat till thick and pale.
4. Add the vanilla and the chocolate mixture and mix till well combined.
5. In another bowl, mix together the flour, cocoa, baking powder and salt.
6. Slowly, add the flour mixture into the chocolate mixture and stir to combine.
7. Fold in the remaining 1 C. of the chocolate chips.
8. Cover the dough and refrigerate to chill for at least an hour or overnight.
9. Set your oven to 350 degrees F.
10. Make about 1-inch balls from the chocolate mixture.
11. Arrange the balls onto ungreased cookie sheets about 2-inches apart.
12. Cook in the oven for about 9-11 minutes.
13. Remove from the oven and let the cookies cool in the cookie sheets for about 5 minutes.
14. Carefully, invert the cookies onto wire rack to cool completely.

3-Ingredient Truffles

Prep Time: 10 mins
Total Time: 1 hr 50 mins

Servings per Recipe: 35
Calories	62 kcal
Fat	4.1 g
Carbohydrates	5.6g
Protein	0.7 g
Cholesterol	4 mg
Sodium	1 mg

Ingredients

- 12 oz. bittersweet chocolate, chopped
- 1/3 C. heavy cream
- 1 tsp vanilla extract

Directions

1. In a medium pan mix together the chocolate and cream on medium heat.
2. Cook, stirring till the chocolate melts and mixture becomes smooth.
3. Remove from the heat and add the flavoring and beat well.
4. Transfer the mixture into a small dish and refrigerate for about 1 1/2 - 2 hours.
5. Make the balls from the mixture and roll in the toppings.

WHITE CHOCOLATE
Truffles

🥣 Prep Time: 5 mins
🕐 Total Time: 30 mins

Servings per Recipe: 16
Calories　　　　96 kcal
Fat　　　　　　5.5 g
Carbohydrates　10.9 g
Protein　　　　1.5 g
Cholesterol　　6 mg
Sodium　　　　34 mg

Ingredients

1 1/3 C. shredded coconut
1/2 C. confectioners' sugar
3 1/2 oz. ricotta cheese
16 whole almonds
2 1/2 (1 oz.) squares white chocolate
2 2/3 tbsp heavy cream

1/4 C. shredded coconut

Directions

1. In a bowl, add 1 1/3 C. of the shredded coconut, sugar and ricotta cheese and mix till a dough-like texture forms.
2. Divide the dough into 16 equal portions.
3. Roll each portion into a ball, pressing one almond into the center of each ball.
4. Freezer for about 20 minutes.
5. In a large stainless steel bowl, add the white chocolate and set over a pan of barely simmering water to melt.
6. While the chocolate is melting, add the heavy cream and stir to combine.
7. With a fork, dip the truffles in the chocolate mixture.
8. Refrigerate till the chocolate coating solidifies.

Shredded Coconut Truffles

Prep Time: 10 mins
Total Time: 1 hr 40 mins

Servings per Recipe: 36
Calories 369 kcal
Fat 20 g
Cholesterol 49.3g
Sodium 3.3 g
Carbohydrates 17 mg
Protein 84 mg

Ingredients

2 (16 oz.) boxes confectioners' sugar
1 (14 oz.) can sweetened condensed milk
1 C. butter
2 1/2 C. chopped walnuts
1 (14 oz.) package shredded coconut
1 (24 oz.) bag chocolate chips

Directions

1. Line a baking sheet with a waxed paper.
2. In a bowl, mix together the sugar, sweetened condensed milk and butter.
3. Stir in the walnuts and coconut in the sugar mixture.
4. With a plastic wrap, cover the bowl and freeze for at least 1 hour.
5. Make about 1-inch balls from the mixture and place on the prepared baking sheet.
6. Freeze for at least 30 minutes.
7. Melt chocolate chips in a double boiler, stirring occasionally till smooth.
8. Coat the balls with the melted chocolate.
9. Place onto the prepared baking sheet and cool till the chocolate has hardened.

ORANGE FRUITCAKE
Truffles

Prep Time: 20 mins
Total Time: 40 mins

Servings per Recipe: 30
Calories	68 kcal
Fat	3.9 g
Carbohydrates	8.2g
Protein	0.6 g
Cholesterol	5 mg
Sodium	20 mg

Ingredients

6 (1 oz.) squares semisweet chocolate, chopped
3 tbsp whipping cream
3 tbsp butter
2 tbsp orange juice
1 C. fruitcake crumbs
1/2 C. sifted confectioners' sugar

Directions

1. In a pan, add the chocolate, cream and butter on very low heat and melt till smooth and well combined.
2. Stir in the juice and fruitcake crumbs.
3. Refrigerate to chill for about 2 hours
4. Make about 1-inch balls from the mixture and refrigerate to chill for at least 20 minutes.
5. Before serving, coat with the icing sugar and refrigerate to chill for about 20 minutes.

Peanut Butter Truffles

Prep Time: 10 mins
Total Time: 43 mins

Servings per Recipe: 25
Calories   70 kcal
Fat   5.7 g
Carbohydrates   4.6 g
Protein   1.5 g
Cholesterol   1 mg
Sodium   25 mg

Ingredients

1/2 C. smooth peanut butter
1/4 C. cocoa powder
1/4 C. honey
1/4 C. coconut oil
1 tsp butter
1 tsp vanilla bean paste
1/4 C. unsweetened coconut flakes

Directions

1. In a pan, mix together the peanut butter, cocoa powder, honey, coconut oil, butter and vanilla bean paste on low heat.
2. Cook, stirring continuously for about 3-5 minutes.
3. Remove from the heat and transfer peanut butter mixture into a bowl.
4. Refrigerate the mixture for about 15 minutes, stirring after every 5 minutes.
5. In a bowl, place the coconut flakes.
6. Place about 1 tsp of the mixture into the coconut and roll to coat.
7. Refrigerate for about 15 minutes.

CREAM CHEESE VANILLA
Truffles

Prep Time: 1 h
Total Time: 1 h

Servings per Recipe: 60
Calories 78 kcal
Fat 3.8 g
Cholesterol 11.7g
Sodium 0.6 g
Carbohydrates 4 mg
Protein 12 mg

Ingredients

1 (8 oz.) package cream cheese, softened
3 C. confectioners' sugar, sifted
3 C. semisweet chocolate chips, melted
1 1/2 tsp vanilla

Directions

1. In a large bowl, add the cream cheese and beat till smooth.
2. Slowly, beat in the confectioners' sugar till well combined.
3. Stir in the melted chocolate and vanilla till no streaks remain.
4. Refrigerate for about 1 hour.
5. Make about 1-inch balls.

Whipped Cream Cookie Truffle Pie

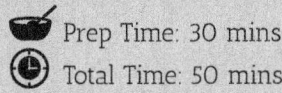 Prep Time: 30 mins
Total Time: 50 mins

Servings per Recipe: 25
Calories 519 kcal
Fat 37.9 g
Carbohydrates 47.4g
Protein 4.1 g
Cholesterol 61 mg
Sodium 209 mg

Ingredients

12 oz. semisweet chocolate chips
1 1/2 C. heavy whipping cream
1/4 C. sifted confectioners' sugar
1 tbsp vanilla extract
1 (9 inch) prepared chocolate cookie crumb crust

Directions

1. In a microwave safe bowl, mix together the chocolate chips and 1/2 of the cream and microwave on high for about 1-2 minutes, stirring after every 30 seconds.
2. Keep aside to cool at room temperature.
3. Stir in the sugar & vanilla.
4. In a small bowl, add the cream and beat till the soft peaks form.
5. Slowly, add the chocolate mixture and beat on high speed till well combined.
6. Place the mixture into the crust.
7. Refrigerate for at least 8 hours before serving.

EXPRESSO
Truffles

Prep Time: 5 mins
Total Time: 1 h 35 mins

Servings per Recipe: 45
Calories	87 kcal
Fat	7.1 g
Carbohydrates	6.8g
Protein	1.2 g
Cholesterol	9 mg
Sodium	6 mg

Ingredients

- 1 C. heavy cream
- 2 tbsp butter
- 4 (1 oz.) squares baking chocolate
- 2 3/4 C. semi-sweet chocolate chips
- 2 tbsp instant espresso powder

Directions

1. In a pan, mix together the heavy cream, butter, baking chocolate, chocolate chips and espresso powder on medium heat.
2. Cook, stirring continuously, till the chocolate is melted into a smooth and thick mixture.
3. Remove from the heat and transfer into a bowl.
4. Refrigerate to chill for about 1 hour.
5. Line a baking sheet with waxed paper.
6. Place the small balls of the chocolate mixture onto the prepared baking sheet.
7. Refrigerate till the balls harden completely.
8. Store in a cool, dry place.

Potluck Truffles

Prep Time: 30 mins
Total Time: 1 hr 30 mins

Servings per Recipe: 200
Calories 47 kcal
Fat 2.3 g
Cholesterol 7g
Sodium 0.4 g
Carbohydrates 2 mg
Protein 7 mg

Ingredients

6 C. semisweet chocolate chips
2 (8 oz.) packages cream cheese, room temperature
6 C. confectioners' sugar
1 tbsp grape juice

Directions

1. Reserve 1/2 C. of the chocolate chips for decoration.
2. Melt the remaining semisweet chocolate in a heatproof bowl over a pan of the barely simmering water, stirring occasionally till melted and smooth.
3. Remove from the heat.
4. In a large bowl, add the cream cheese and with an electric mixer, beat till soft and fluffy.
5. Slowly, add the confectioners' sugar, beating continuously till well combined.
6. Stir in the melted chocolate and juice.
7. Refrigerate, covered for about 1 hour.
8. Make about 3/4-inch balls from the mixture and arrange on a wax paper lined baking sheet.
9. In a microwave safe bowl, melt the reserved chocolate chips till smooth.
10. Drizzle the melted chocolate over the truffles.

MEDITERRANEAN
Almond Truffles

Prep Time: 20 mins
Total Time: 1 h 30 mins

Servings per Recipe: 12
Calories	337 kcal
Fat	17.4 g
Carbohydrates	50.1g
Protein	7.3 g
Cholesterol	0 mg
Sodium	209 mg

Ingredients

1 1/4 C. shredded unsweetened coconut, or to taste, divided
2 C. pitted Medjool dates
1 C. raw almonds
2 1/4 C. raw cocoa powder
1/2 C. cocoa nibs

1/2 C. agave nectar
2 tsp vanilla extract
1 tsp salt

Directions

1. Set your oven to 350 degrees F before doing anything else.
2. In a baking sheet, place the coconut and cook in the oven for about 7 minutes, stirring occasionally.
3. In a food processor, add the dates and almonds and pulse till smooth.
4. Add the cocoa powder and pulse till well combined.
5. Transfer the date mixture into a bowl.
6. Fold 1 C. of the toasted coconut, cocoa nibs, agave nectar, vanilla extract and salt into date mixture.
7. With 1 tbsp of the mixture, make the balls.
8. In a shallow dish, place the remaining toasted coconut.
9. Coat the truffle balls with the toasted coconut and arrange on the parchment lined baking sheet.
10. Refrigerate for about 1 hour.

December's Peppermint Truffles

Prep Time: 30 mins
Total Time: 50 mins

Servings per Recipe: 24
Calories   134 kcal
Fat   9 g
Cholesterol   14.3g
Sodium   1.2 g
Carbohydrates   7 mg
Protein   10 mg

Ingredients

11 oz. chocolate, chopped
1/2 C. heavy whipping cream
1 1/2 C. chopped peppermint crunch thin mints (such as Andes(R))

Directions

1. Melt the chocolate and cream in the top of a double boiler over simmering water without stirring for 3 minutes.
2. Beat the chocolate and cream till smooth.
3. Remove from the heat and keep aside to cool for about 20-30 minutes.
4. In a flat baking sheet, place the chocolate mixture.
5. With a plastic wrap, cover the baking sheet and refrigerate to chill for about 3 hours.
6. In a shallow bowl, place the chopped peppermint candies.
7. With about 1 1/2 tsp of chocolate mixture, make the balls and arrange on a piece of parchment paper lined baking sheet.
8. Coat the truffles with the peppermint candy and lightly roll truffles between your hands to press the candy pieces into truffles.

SIMPLE
Truffle Torte

🥣 Prep Time: 15 mins
🕐 Total Time: 4 h 17 mins

Servings per Recipe: 16
Calories   254 kcal
Fat   21.2 g
Carbohydrates   16.7g
Protein   3.6 g
Cholesterol   100 mg
Sodium   111 mg

Ingredients

2 1/2 C. semi-sweet chocolate chips
1 C. butter
6 large eggs

Directions

1. Set your oven to 425 degrees F before doing anything else.
2. Fill a 12-inch baking pan with 1-inch of the water and place water bath in the oven while heating.
3. Grease a 9-inch spring form pan and line with buttered parchment paper and with foil, wrap the outside of the pan.
4. In a large microwave safe bowl, add the chocolate chips and butter and microwave on the Defrost setting for about 1 minute.
5. Stir and continue heating in microwave for about 1 to 2 minutes more.
6. Set a large bowl over a pot of simmering water over medium-low heat and cook and stir eggs in the large bowl till just warm. Remove from heat and beat using an electric mixer until triple the volume and soft peaks form, about 5 minutes.
7. With a rubber spatula, fold 1/2 of the eggs into the chocolate mixture.
8. Fold in the remaining eggs till just combined.
9. Place the mixture into the prepared spring form pan evenly.
10. Arrange the spring form pan in the water bath in the oven.
11. Cook in the oven for about 5 minutes.
12. With some foil, cover the pan loosely and cook for about 10 minutes more.
13. Remove from the oven and cool on a wire rack for about 45 minutes.
14. Cover with plastic wrap and refrigerate for about 3 hours to overnight.

Raisins, Cranberry, and Plum Truffles

Prep Time: 20 mins
Total Time: 40 mins

Servings per Recipe: 36
Calories   55 kcal
Fat   3.1 g
Carbohydrates   7g
Protein   0.9 g
Cholesterol   1 mg
Sodium   1 mg

Ingredients

1 1/2 C. walnuts
1 C. orange-essence dried plums (prunes)
1/2 C. dried cranberries
1/2 C. plain raisins
1 tsp cinnamon
1/4 tsp ground ginger
1 tsp vanilla extract

Directions

1. In a food processor, add all the ingredients and pulse till the mixture forms into a dough-like ball.
2. With your hands, roll the mixture into 1-inch balls.
3. Coat the balls with the coconut.

I ♥ Truffles

Prep Time: 15 mins
Total Time: 1 h 25 mins

Servings per Recipe: 24
Calories   152 kcal
Fat   11.3 g
Carbohydrates   14.6g
Protein   1 g
Cholesterol   19 mg
Sodium   20 mg

Ingredients

1 C. heavy cream
1/4 C. white sugar
1/4 C. butter
1 (16 oz.) package semisweet chocolate chips
1 tbsp hazelnut coffee creamer

Directions

1. In a pan, add the heavy cream and sugar on medium heat and beat well.
2. Heat till the sugar is dissolved, stirring continuously.
3. Remove from the heat and add the butter, chocolate chips and Irish cream and beat till the butter and chocolate chips are melted completely.
4. Keep aside to cool at room temperature.
5. Make about 1-inch balls from the mixture and arrange the truffles on a plate.
6. Refrigerate for about 1 hour.

Raspberry Truffle Fudge

Prep Time: 10 mins
Total Time: 1 hr 20 mins

Servings per Recipe: 40
Calories   149 kcal
Fat   7.5 g
Carbohydrates   19.7g
Protein   2.3 g
Cholesterol   5 mg
Sodium   13 mg

Ingredients

3 C. semi-sweet chocolate chips
1 (14 oz.) can sweetened condensed milk
1 1/2 tsp vanilla extract
salt to taste
1/4 C. heavy cream
1/4 C. fruit juice
2 C. semi-sweet chocolate chips

Directions

1. Grease a 9x9-inch baking dish with the non-stick cooking spray and line with a wax paper.
2. In a microwave-safe bowl, mix together 3 C. of the chocolate chips and sweetened condensed milk and microwave until chocolate melts, stirring occasionally.
3. Stir in the vanilla and salt.
4. Transfer the mixture into the pan and cool at room temperature.
5. In a microwave-safe bowl, mix together the cream, juice and 2 C. of the chocolate chips and microwave till the chocolate melts.
6. Cool the mixture to lukewarm, then place over the fudge layer.
7. Refrigerate for at least 1 hour.
8. Cut into 1-inch pieces.

APRICOT CINNAMON
Truffles

Prep Time: 20 mins
Total Time: 50 mins

Servings per Recipe: 36
Calories	59 kcal
Fat	3.5 g
Carbohydrates	6.4g
Protein	1.5 g
Cholesterol	0 mg
Sodium	4 mg

Ingredients

- 1 1/2 C. whole, unsalted almonds
- 2 C. dried apricots
- 2 tsp cinnamon
- 2 tsp almond extract
- 1/2 C. sweetened shredded coconut

Directions

1. In a food processor, add all the ingredients except the coconut and pulse till the mixture forms into a dough-like ball.
2. With your hands, roll the mixture into 1-inch balls.
3. Coat the balls with the coconut.

Southern Jam Truffles

Prep Time: 30 mins
Total Time: 5 hr 35 mins

Servings per Recipe: 36
Calories	96 kcal
Fat	5.7 g
Carbohydrates	11.8g
Protein	1 g
Cholesterol	7 mg
Sodium	31 mg

Ingredients

- 1 C. semisweet chocolate chips
- 1 (8 oz.) package cream cheese, softened
- 3/4 C. crushed vanilla wafers
- 1/2 C. seedless raspberry jam
- 1 C. semisweet chocolate chips

Directions

1. In a microwave safe bowl, add the chocolate chips and microwave on Low in 30-second intervals, stirring after each melting, till the chocolate is smooth for about 1-3 minutes.
2. Add the cream cheese into the melted chocolate and beat till smooth.
3. Stir in the wafer crumbs and raspberry jam.
4. Refrigerate, covered for about 4 hours.
5. Make about 1-inch balls from the mixture and place on a baking sheet.
6. Freeze for about 1 hour.
7. In a microwave safe bowl, add the remaining 1 C. of the chocolate chips and microwave on Low for about 1-3 minutes, stirring after every 30 seconds.
8. Dip the frozen chocolate balls into the melted chocolate and keep aside to set before serving.

HAZELNUT
Truffle Cupcakes

Prep Time: 20 mins
Total Time: 45 mins

Servings per Recipe: 24
Calories   345 kcal
Fat   18.9 g
Carbohydrates   39.3g
Protein   5.2 g
Cholesterol   44 mg
Sodium   135 mg

Ingredients

2 1/4 C. all-purpose flour
1/2 C. unsweetened cocoa powder
1 tbsp baking powder
3/4 C. milk
1/4 C. strong brewed coffee
1 tsp vanilla extract

1 C. butter
1 1/2 C. white sugar
3 eggs, at room temperature
24 chocolate-hazelnut truffles
1 (13 oz.) jar chocolate-hazelnut spread
1/4 C. chopped hazelnuts

Directions

1. Set your oven to 350 degrees F before doing anything else and line a muffin pan with paper liners.
2. In a bowl, sift together the flour, cocoa and baking powder.
3. In a second small bowl, mix together the milk, coffee and vanilla.
4. In a third large bowl, add the butter and sugar and with an electric mixer, beat till light and fluffy.
5. Add the eggs one at a time, beating till well combined.
6. Add the flour mixture alternately with the milk mixture, mixing till just combined.
7. Place half of the mixture into the prepared cups evenly.
8. Place an unwrapped truffle into the cup and press in the bottom and spread the remaining flour mixture over the top of each truffle.
9. Cook in the oven for about 20-25 minutes.
10. Remove from the oven and let the cupcakes cool in the pan for about 5-10 minutes.
11. Carefully, invert the cupcakes onto wire rack to cool completely.
12. Spread the chocolate-hazelnut spread over the cupcakes and garnish with chopped hazelnuts.

Carolina Sunflower Truffles

Prep Time: 10 mins
Total Time: 35 mins

Servings per Recipe: 32
Calories   176 kcal
Fat   17.1 g
Cholesterol   8.7g
Sodium   1 g
Carbohydrates   0 mg
Protein   29 mg

Ingredients

Chocolate:
2 C. coconut oil, melted
1 C. unsweetened cocoa powder
1/2 C. raw honey, melted
2 tbsp stevia powder
Strawberry Filling:
3/4 C. strawberries
1/4 C. coconut oil
1/4 C. sunflower seed butter
2 tbsp raw honey
1/2 lemon, juiced
1 vanilla bean, split lengthwise and seeds scraped
1/4 tsp Himalayan rock salt

Directions

1. In a bowl, add 2 C. of the coconut oil, cocoa powder, 1/2 C. of the honey and stevia powder and beat till smooth.
2. In a food processor, add the strawberries, 1/4 C. of the coconut oil, sunflower seed butter, 2 tbsp of the honey, lemon juice, vanilla bean seeds and rock salt and pulse till smooth.
3. Transfer the mixture into a bowl and refrigerate.
4. Place about half of the chocolate mixture into the bottoms of truffle molds and freeze for about 10 minutes.
5. Keep the remaining chocolate aside at room temperature.
6. Place about 1 1/2 tsp to 1 tbsp of the strawberry filling over the frozen chocolate and top with the remaining chocolate.
7. Freeze the truffles for about 15 minutes.

PECAN
Truffles

Prep Time: 8 mins
Total Time: 4 hr

Servings per Recipe: 12
Calories   195 kcal
Fat   12.8 g
Carbohydrates   21.2g
Protein   2.1 g
Cholesterol   10 mg
Sodium   23 mg

Ingredients

1/2 C. chopped pecans
1/2 C. granulated sugar
6 tbsp heavy cream
9 (1 oz.) squares semi-sweet baking chocolate, divided
1/8 tsp Diamond Crystal(R) Kosher Salt
1/2 tsp vanilla extract

Directions

1. In a dry skillet, add the pecans on medium heat and toast for about 1 minute.
2. Keep aside to cool.
3. In a heavy pan, add the sugar on medium-high heat and cook, stirring continuously till the sugar begins to melt.
4. Remove the caramelized sugar from the heat and stir in the cream.
5. Return to heat and reduce the heat to low.
6. Cook and stir till the caramel is dissolved completely in the cream.
7. Remove from the heat and add the salt, vanilla and half of the chocolate and stir till the chocolate melts completely.
8. Stir in the toasted pecan bits.
9. Transfer the mixture into a bowl and cool slightly.
10. Refrigerate, covered for about an hour.
11. Make 24 (3/4-inch) balls from the mixture and arrange on a parchment-lined baking sheet.
12. Refrigerate to chill for about 1 hour.
13. In a microwave-safe bowl, place the remaining chocolate and microwave on High in 15-second intervals, stirring after each melting, till the chocolate is melted.
14. With a fork, coat the balls in the melted chocolate and place back on the parchment-lined bake sheet.
15. Immediately, sprinkle truffles with a few grains of salt.
16. Refrigerate to chill for about 1 hour.

Moe's Favorite
Truffles

Prep Time: 15 mins
Total Time: 3 hr 50 mins

Servings per Recipe: 24
Calories   99 kcal
Fat   6.4 g
Carbohydrates   10.8g
Protein   1.5 g
Cholesterol   5 mg
Sodium   8 mg

Ingredients

12 oz. semisweet chocolate
1 banana, mashed
1/3 C. heavy whipping cream
2 tbsp peanut butter
1/4 C. sifted confectioners' sugar, or as needed

Directions

1. In a pan, mix together the chocolate, banana, cream and peanut butter on medium heat and cook, stirring for about 5-10 minutes.
2. Transfer the mixture into a bowl and refrigerate for about 2 1/2-3 hours.
3. In a shallow dish, place the confectioners' sugar.
4. With a melon baller, make about 1-inch balls and coat with the confectioners' sugar evenly.
5. Refrigerate for about 1-2 hours.

ALMOND BARK
Truffles

Prep Time: 30 mins
Total Time: 3 hr 30 mins

Servings per Recipe: 50
Calories	160 kcal
Fat	9.9 g
Cholesterol	19.1g
Sodium	2.5 g
Carbohydrates	8 mg
Protein	25 mg

Ingredients

3/4 C. firmly packed brown sugar
1/2 C. butter, softened
1 tsp vanilla extract
2 C. all-purpose flour
1 (14 oz.) can sweetened condensed milk
1/2 C. miniature semisweet chocolate chips
1 C. finely chopped pecans
1 1/2 lb. chocolate almond bark (chocolate confectioners' coating)

Directions

1. Line the baking sheets with the waxed papers.
2. In a large bowl, add the brown sugar and butter and with an electric mixer, beat till smooth and creamy.
3. Add the vanilla extract and beat till smooth.
4. Slowly, add the flour into the cream butter mixture, beating continuously till smooth.
5. Add the sweetened condensed milk and beat till smooth.
6. Make about 1-inch balls from the mixture and place onto the prepared baking sheets.
7. Refrigerate the cookie dough balls for about 2 hours.
8. Melt chocolate bark in the top of a double boiler over simmering water, stirring frequently and scraping down the sides with a rubber spatula to avoid scorching.
9. Coat each ball with the melted chocolate.
10. Place dipped balls onto the waxed paper and refrigerate to chill for at least 1 hour.

Chive Truffles

🥣 Prep Time: 20 mins
🕒 Total Time: 30 mins

Servings per Recipe: 13
Calories   84 kcal
Fat   6.9 g
Cholesterol   2.4g
Sodium   3.4 g
Carbohydrates   12 mg
Protein   88 mg

Ingredients

4 oz. chevre, crumbled
2 oz. cream cheese, softened
2 tbsp apple juice
Salt and pepper to taste
13 grapes
1/2 C. whole almonds
1/4 C. thinly sliced chives

Directions

1. In a bowl, add the chevre and cream cheese and with a fork, mix well.
2. Add the juice and a pinch of salt and pepper and mix till smooth.
3. Refrigerate to chill for about 30 minutes.
4. In a dry frying, add the almonds on medium-high heat and toast, shaking the pan frequently for about 5 minutes.
5. Transfer onto a large cutting board to cool.
6. With a chef's knife, chop the almonds finely.
7. Take about 1 tbsp of the cheese mixture and press 1 grape inside.
8. Roll the mixture into little ball.
9. Repeat with the remaining mixture.
10. In a shallow dish, mix together the almonds and chives.
11. Coat each truffle ball with the almonds mixture evenly.
12. Refrigerate, covered until serving.

NUTELLA
Truffles

Prep Time: 25 mins
Total Time: 12 hr 40 mins

Servings per Recipe: 28
Calories	135 kcal
Fat	8 g
Carbohydrates	16.9 g
Protein	1.6 g
Cholesterol	8 mg
Sodium	219 mg

Ingredients

- 1 C. chocolate-hazelnut spread
- 1/3 C. white sugar
- 2 tbsp water
- 2/3 C. heavy whipping cream
- 1/4 tsp coarse sea salt
- 1/2 C. unsweetened cocoa powder
- 1 (12 oz.) bag chocolate chips (at least cocoa), finely chopped
- 1 tbsp coarse sea salt (such as Diamond Crystal(R)), or to taste

Directions

1. Add the hazelnut spread in metal bowl over a pan of gently simmering water and stir till the hazelnut spread is warm and smooth for about 5 minutes.
2. Remove the bowl from the heat.
3. In a small pan, add the sugar and water on medium heat and stir till dissolved.
4. Brush the sides of the pan with a moistened pastry brush occasionally as the sugar mixture cooks.
5. Increase the heat to medium-high and bring syrup to a boil and cook for about 4 minutes, brushing down sides and swirling the pan occasionally to prevent scorching.
6. Add the cream into the syrup, stirring continuously.
7. Reduce the heat to low and cook, stirring continuously for about 5-10 minutes.
8. Gently stir in 1/4 tsp of salt into the melted hazelnut spread.
9. Refrigerate caramel mixture for at least 3 hours.
10. In a shallow dish, place the cocoa powder.
11. With about 1 tbsp of the mixture, make the balls and coat with the cocoa powder.
12. Arrange the balls onto a baking sheet.
13. With a plastic wrap, cover truffle balls and refrigerate to chill for about 8 hours.

14. Line a 13x9-inch baking sheet with foil.
15. Heat chopped chocolate in a metal bowl set over a saucepan of gently simmering water, stirring frequently until chocolate is melted and smooth.
16. Remove the bowl from the pan of water.
17. Working quickly, dip each truffle ball in the melted chocolate.
18. With a fork, lift the truffles from the chocolate and tap fork against side of bowl to remove excess coating.
19. Transfer the truffles to foil-lined pan to cool.
20. Sprinkle the finished truffles lightly with 1 tbsp of the coarse sea salt before the chocolate hardens.
21. Keep aside for at least 1 hour before serving.

VENUS
Truffles

🥣 Prep Time: 1 hr 30 mins
🕐 Total Time: 2 hr

Servings per Recipe: 60
Calories   99 kcal
Fat   5 g
Cholesterol   12.4g
Sodium   0.9 g
Carbohydrates   5 mg
Protein   14 mg

Ingredients

12 oz. high quality dark chocolate, chopped
16 oz. canned whole chestnuts, drained
6 tbsp butter, softened
1/2 C. white sugar
1/4 C. brandy

1 tsp vanilla extract
12 oz. high quality white chocolate, chopped - divided
1 dash powdered red food coloring

Directions

1. Place the dark chocolate into the top part of a double boiler over the simmering water and melt the chocolate.
2. Remove from the heat and let the chocolate cool.
3. In a food processor, add the chestnuts and pulse till a smoothly puree forms.
4. In a bowl, add the butter and sugar and with an electric mixer, beat till the mixture is light and fluffy.
5. Add the chestnuts puree, brandy and vanilla extract and mix till the mixture becomes smooth.
6. Stir in the chocolate.
7. Refrigerate the mixture for several hours.
8. Make about 1-inch sized balls from the mixture.
9. Reserve about 1 oz. of the white chocolate for the tempering and about 1 oz. for the coloring.
10. Add the remaining 10 oz. of the white chocolate over simmering water in a double boiler till the chocolate is melted and warm but not hot.
11. Remove the pan from the double boiler.
12. Immediately, add about 1 oz. of the chopped, unmelted white chocolate and stir the till the

unmelted pieces of chocolate melt.
13. Carefully dip the center of each ball in the melted white chocolate and gently place the truffle onto a piece of parchment paper for about 15 minutes.
14. Melt the remaining 1 oz. of chopped white chocolate over simmering water in a double boiler till the chocolate is melted and warm but not hot.
15. Stir in a very small amount of powdered red food coloring until you get a desired shade of pink.
16. Dip a little colored chocolate out with a spoon, dot each truffle with a pink dot and allow the pink chocolate dots to set for about 15 minutes.
17. Place the truffles into paper candy cups to serve.

TRUE ITALIAN
Truffles

🥣 Prep Time: 20 mins
🕐 Total Time: 1 d 2 h 40 m

Servings per Recipe: 8
Calories	394 kcal
Fat	24.4 g
Carbohydrates	39.4g
Protein	5.8 g
Cholesterol	150 mg
Sodium	57 mg

Ingredients

Chocolate-Hazelnut Gelato:
2 C. whole milk
1 C. heavy cream
1/3 C. white sugar
4 egg yolks
1/3 C. white sugar

1/2 C. chocolate-hazelnut spread
2 tbsp instant espresso powder
1/2 tsp vanilla extract
3 oz. fine quality bittersweet chocolate, finely chopped
8 maraschino cherries
frozen whipped topping, thawed

Directions

1. In a pan, add the milk, cream, and 1/3 C. on medium heat.
2. Cook, stirring continuously for about 3-5 minutes.
3. In a bowl, add the egg yolks and 1/3 C. of the sugar and beat till the egg yolks become light in color.
4. Add 1/2 C. of the milk mixture into the egg yolks and stir to combine.
5. Transfer the milk mixture into the pan, stirring continuously.
6. Cook, stirring continuously for about 8-10 minutes.
7. Remove from the heat.
8. Add the chocolate hazelnut spread, espresso powder and vanilla, stirring till well combined.
9. Strain through a mesh strainer into a bowl.
10. Refrigerate several hours till cold.
11. Transfer the mixture into an ice cream maker and freeze according to manufacturer's directions.
12. Transfer gelato into an airtight container and place in freezer until solid.
13. To make a tartufo, scoop 4-oz. portions of gelato and make the balls with your hands.
14. With a fork, poke a hole in each ball and place 1 cherry inside.

15. Cover with the gelato and place on a baking sheet.
16. Coat the gelato balls with the grated chocolate evenly and freeze before serving.
17. Serve with whipped topping.

TRUFFLED
Cheesecake

Prep Time: 15 mins
Total Time: 1 h 20 mins

Servings per Recipe: 8
Calories	1018 kcal
Fat	64.3 g
Carbohydrates	76.2g
Protein	15.5 g
Cholesterol	223 mg
Sodium	517 mg

Ingredients

Chocolate Crumb Crust:
1 1/2 C. vanilla wafer crumbs
6 tbsp powdered sugar
1/3 C. unsweetened cocoa powder
1/3 C. butter, melted
Filling:

3 (8 oz.) packages cream cheese, softened
1 (14 oz.) can Sweetened Condensed Milk
2 C. semi-sweet chocolate chips, melted*
4 large eggs
2 tsp vanilla extract

Directions

1. Set your oven to 300 degrees F before doing anything else.
2. In a bowl, mix together the wafer crumbs, powdered sugar, cocoa.
3. In the bottom and 1/2 inch up side of 1 ungreased 9-inch spring form pan, place the mixture and firmly press downwards.
4. In another bowl, add the cream cheese and beat till fluffy.
5. Slowly, add the sweetened condensed milk, beating continuously till smooth.
6. Add remaining ingredients and mix well.
7. Place over the crumb mixture into the pan.
8. Cook in the oven for about 65 minutes.
9. Remove from the oven and cool completely.
10. Refrigerate to chill.
11. Garnish as desired.

Gourmet Truffles

Prep Time: 25 mins
Total Time: 30 mins

Servings per Recipe: 25
Calories   264 kcal
Fat   17.6 g
Carbohydrates   25.4 g
Protein   2.7 g
Cholesterol   32 mg
Sodium   214 mg

Ingredients

6 C. graham cracker crumbs
1 1/2 C. butter, melted
1 C. milk chocolate or semisweet chocolate chips
1 C. flaked sweetened coconut

Directions

1. In a bowl, add the graham cracker crumbs and melted butter and mix till well moistened.
2. In a microwave-safe glass bowl, melt the chocolate chips in 30-second intervals, stirring after each melting, for about 1-3 minutes.
3. Add the melted chocolate into the graham cracker mixture and with your hand, mix till well combined.
4. Make about 1-inch balls and coat them with the coconut.
5. Store in an airtight container.

GLAMOROUS
★Truffles★

Prep Time: 10 mins
Total Time: 3 hr

Servings per Recipe: 72
Calories	53 kcal
Fat	2.5 g
Cholesterol	7.5g
Sodium	0.9 g
Carbohydrates	2 mg
Protein	7 mg

Ingredients

3 C. semi-sweet chocolate chips
1 (14 oz.) can sweetened condensed milk
1 tbsp vanilla extract

Directions

1. In large pan, melt the chocolate chips with the sweetened condensed milk.
2. Remove from the heat and stir in the vanilla.
3. Transfer the mixture into a medium bowl.
4. Refrigerate, covered to hill for about 2-3 hours.
5. Make about 1-inch balls from the mixture and coat with the desired covering.
6. Refrigerate in a tightly covered dish.

Restaurant Style Truffles

🥣 Prep Time: 1 hr 30 mins
🕐 Total Time: 1 hr 30 mins

Servings per Recipe: 48
Calories 146 kcal
Fat 7.9 g
Cholesterol 19.3g
Sodium 2.1 g
Carbohydrates 10 mg
Protein 38 mg

Ingredients

- 1/2 C. butter, softened
- 3/4 C. packed brown sugar
- 1 tsp vanilla extract
- 2 1/4 C. all-purpose flour
- 1 (14 oz.) can sweetened condensed milk
- 1/2 C. miniature semisweet chocolate chips
- 1/2 C. toffee baking bits
- 1 lb. chocolate confectioners' coating

Directions

1. In a large bowl, add the brown sugar and butter and with an electric mixer, beat till smooth.
2. Stir in the vanilla extract.
3. Slowly, add the flour, alternately with sweetened condensed milk, beating well after each addition.
4. Gently, fold in the chocolate chips and toffee bits.
5. With a small cookie scoop, make 1-inch balls and arrange on waxed paper lined baking sheets.
6. Refrigerate for about 1 hour.
7. In a microwave-safe glass bowl, melt the chocolate coating in 30-second intervals, stirring after each melting, for about 1-3 minutes
8. Dip the dough balls in the chocolate coating, discarding any excess.
9. Arrange on waxed-paper lined baking sheets and sprinkle the truffles with the additional toffee pieces.
10. Refrigerate until firm, about 15 minutes. Store in the refrigerator.

FRENCH
Truffles

Prep Time: 20 mins
Total Time: 2 h 30 mins

Servings per Recipe: 12
Calories 108 kcal
Fat 8.2 g
Cholesterol 9.2g
Sodium 1.5 g
Carbohydrates 12 mg
Protein 3 mg

Ingredients

1/3 C. heavy whipping cream
1/2 tsp vanilla extract
1 pinch salt
2 tbsp apple juice, optional
6 (1 oz.) squares semisweet chocolate, chopped

1 tbsp unsalted butter, room temperature
1/4 C. unsweetened cocoa powder

Directions

1. In a pan, mix together the cream, vanilla extract and salt and bring to a boil.
2. Stir in the juice and remove from the heat.
3. Add the semisweet chocolate and butter in the cream mixture and mix till melted completely.
4. Transfer the chocolate mixture into a container.
5. With a plastic wrap, cover and refrigerate for at least 2 hours.
6. Line 2 baking sheets with parchment paper.
7. With a tsp, make about 1-inch balls and arrange on the prepared baking sheets.
8. Refrigerate for about 10 minutes.
9. Remove from the refrigerator and coat the balls with the cocoa powder.

Truffle Icing

Prep Time: 10 mins
Total Time: 20 mins

Servings per Recipe: 12
Calories	52 kcal
Fat	1.3 g
Cholesterol	10.8g
Sodium	0.4 g
Carbohydrates	1 mg
Protein	2 mg

Ingredients

1 C. confectioners' sugar
2 tbsp milk
1 (1 oz.) square unsweetened chocolate, melted

Directions

1. In a bowl, add the sugar, milk and unsweetened chocolate and mix till smooth.
2. This icing can be used for dipping the truffle cookies.

TRUFFLES
Forever

Prep Time: 30 mins
Total Time: 1 hr 10 mins

Servings per Recipe: 50
Calories   73 kcal
Fat   4.5 g
Carbohydrates   8.3g
Protein   0.8 g
Cholesterol   3 mg
Sodium   7 mg

Ingredients

cooking spray
12 oz. milk chocolate
1/3 C. light cream
1 tsp vanilla extract
12 oz. semisweet chocolate chips
2 tsp shortening

Directions

1. Line a baking sheet with a greased wax paper.
2. In a small pan, add the milk chocolate on low heat and melt, stirring continuously.
3. Stir in the cream and vanilla.
4. Place about tbsp-sized scoops of the chocolate mixture onto the prepared baking sheet and refrigerate for about 30 minutes.
5. In a small pan, melt the chocolate chips on low heat.
6. Add the shortening and stir to combine.
7. Roll each piece of the chilled chocolate into a ball.
8. Coat the chocolate balls with the melted chocolate chip mixture.
9. Arrange the truffles onto the prepared baking sheet and refrigerate to chill till firm.

TRUFFLES
Combo

Prep Time: 30 mins
Total Time: 1 hr

Servings per Recipe: 30
Calories	73 kcal
Fat	4.8 g
Carbohydrates	6.6g
Protein	2.2 g
Cholesterol	3 mg
Sodium	68 mg

Ingredients

10 slices turkey bacon
8 (1 oz.) squares semisweet chocolate
2 bananas, peeled
5 tbsp smooth peanut butter, divided

Directions

1. Heat a large skillet on medium-high heat and cook the bacon for about 10 minutes.
2. Transfer the bacon onto a paper towel lined plate to drain and cut into 1-inch pieces.
3. Melt 2/3 of the chocolate in the top of a double boiler over the barely simmering water, stirring till the chocolate is melted completely.
4. Stir in the remaining chopped chocolate.
5. Remove from the heat and stir till the temperature of the chocolate comes down to 88-90 F degrees and most of the chocolate pieces have melted.
6. Discard any unmelted pieces and hold the chocolate over warm water for dipping.
7. Slice the each banana into 1-inch pieces and cut each piece down the center to make half-moons.
8. Spread the bottom of each half-moon with about 1/2 tsp of peanut butter.
9. Stick the banana piece, peanut butter side down onto a square of bacon and skewer the banana and bacon together with a toothpick.
10. Coat the banana and bacon treats with the melted chocolate evenly.
11. Arrange the dipped treats onto parchment paper to cool and set.

Fathia's Truffles

🥣 Prep Time: 40 mins
🕐 Total Time: 5 hr 30 mins

Servings per Recipe: 12
Calories	159 kcal
Fat	12.4 g
Carbohydrates	11.8g
Protein	1.5 g
Cholesterol	15 mg
Sodium	2 mg

Ingredients

- 1/4 C. unsalted butter
- 3 tbsp heavy cream
- 4 (1 oz.) squares semisweet chocolate, chopped
- 2 tbsp orange juice
- 1 tsp grated orange zest
- 4 (1 oz.) squares semisweet chocolate, chopped
- 1 tbsp vegetable oil

Directions

1. In a medium pan, mix together the butter and cream on medium-high heat and bring to a boil.
2. Remove from the heat and add 4 oz. of the chopped chocolate, orange juice and orange zest and stir till smooth.
3. Place the truffle mixture into a 9X5-inch loaf pan and refrigerate to chill for about 2 hours.
4. Line a baking sheet with waxed paper.
5. With a rounded tsp, make small balls from the mixture and arrange onto the prepared baking sheet.
6. Refrigerate to chill for about 30 minutes.
7. In the top of a double boiler over lightly simmering water, melt the remaining 4 oz. of the chocolate with the oil, stirring till smooth.
8. Remove from the heat and keep aside to cool till lukewarm.
9. Place the truffles, one at a time into the melted chocolate mixture and coat evenly.
10. Arrange the truffles onto baking sheet and refrigerate to chill till set.

ENJOY THE RECIPES?

KEEP ON COOKING WITH 6 MORE FREE COOKBOOKS!

Click the link below and simply enter your email address to join the club and receive your 6 cookbooks.

http://booksumo.com/magnet

https://www.instagram.com/booksumopress/

https://www.facebook.com/booksumo/

Printed in Great Britain
by Amazon